THE BROTHERS SIZE

BY TARELL ALVIN McCRANEY

DRAMATISTS
PLAY SERVICE
INC.

NOTE ON BILLING

Anyone receiving permission to produce THE BROTHERS SIZE is required to give credit to the Author as sole and exclusive Author of the Play on the title page of all programs distributed in connection with performances of the Play and in all instances in which the title of the Play appears, including printed or digital materials for advertising, publicizing or otherwise exploiting the Play and/or a production thereof. The name of the Author must appear on a separate line, in which no other name appears, immediately beneath the title and in size of type equal to 50% of the size of the largest, most prominent letter used for the title of the Play. No person, firm or entity may receive credit larger or more prominent than that accorded the Author. The following acknowledgments must appear on the title page of all programs distributed in connection with performances of the Play, and in all advertising and publicity in which full production credits appear:

World premiere of THE BROTHERS SIZE produced by the Foundry Theater
(Melanie Joseph, Producing Artistic Director)
and the Public Theater
(Oskar Eustis, Artistic Director; Mara Manus, Executive Director).

U.K. stage premiere produced by the Young Vic Company.

World premiere of THE BROTHER/SISTER PLAYS produced by the Public Theater
(Oskar Eustis, Artistic Director; Andrew D. Hamingson, Executive Director),
and McCarter Theatre Center
(Emily Mann, Artistic Director; Timothy J. Shields, Managing Director).

THE BROTHER/SISTER PLAYS were developed
with the support of McCarter Theatre Center.

THE BROTHERS SIZE received its world premiere at the Mc-Carter Theatre in Princeton, New Jersey, on May 22, 2009. It was directed by Robert O'Hara; the set design was by James Schuette; the costume design was by Karen Perry; the lighting design was by Jane Cox; the sound design was by Lindsay Jones; and the production stage manager was Cheryl Mintz. The cast was as follows:

OGUN SIZE .... Marc Damon Johnson
OSHOOSI SIZE .... Brian Tyree Henry
ELEGBA .... André Holland

CHARACTERS

OGUN (Oh Goon) HENRI SIZE, late 20s, a man of color, auto mechanic.

OSHOOSI (O Chew See) SIZE, early 20s, a man of color, ex-con, out on parole, younger brother to Ogun.

ELEGBA, (Eh Leg Bah) also ex-con, prisonmate and best friend of Oshoosi. Late 20s as well, of Creole heritage.

PLACE

San Pere, Louisiana near the bayou.

TIME

Distant present.

NOTES

THE BROTHERS SIZE draws on elements, icons, and stories from the Yoruba cosmology.

Stage directions written as dialogue under character names are to be spoken as well as played. Stage directions written in parenthesis are to be played only.

Italicized words are songs.

If there is a space after a character name, it means there is a silent action or pause being played at that moment.

A man that hath friends must show himself friendly:
and there is a friend that sticketh closer than a brother.

—Proverbs 18, Verse 24

THE BROTHERS SIZE

Prologue

The Opening Song

Lights come up on the three men standing onstage. This is the opening invocation and should be repeated for as long as needed to complete the ritual.

OGUN SIZE.
Ogun Size stands in the early morning, with a shovel in his hand. He begins his work on the driveway, huh!
OSHOOSI SIZE.
Oshoosi Size is in his bed sleeping. He stirs, dreaming, a very bad dream, mmm …
ELEGBA.
Elegba enters, drifting, like the moon. Singing a song.
OGUN SIZE.
Sharp breath out
ELEGBA.
This road is rough …
OSHOOSI SIZE.
Mmmm …
OGUN SIZE.
Huh!
ELEGBA.
This road is rough.
OSHOOSI SIZE.
Mmm …

OGUN SIZE.
   Huh!
ELEGBA.
   This road is rough and
OGUN SIZE.
   Good God!
ELEGBA.
   It's rough and hard
OGUN SIZE.
   Lord God!
ELEGBA.
   It's rough …
OSHOOSI SIZE.
   Mmm …
OGUN SIZE.
   Huh!
ELEGBA.
   Lord God
   it's rough.
OSHOOSI SIZE.
   Mmm …
OGUN SIZE.
   Huh!
ELEGBA.
   This road is rough. Yeah, this road is rough.
OGUN SIZE.
   (Breath out!)

ACT ONE

Scene 1

OGUN SIZE.
> Ogun Size enters. Osi!
> Calling for his brother Osi ... Oshoosi!

OSHOOSI SIZE.
> Waking from his dream! What man, what?

OGUN SIZE.
> Get up.

OSHOOSI SIZE.
> Nigga comin' in here turning on lights!

OGUN SIZE.
> That's the sun.

OSHOOSI SIZE.
> Kissing his teeth

OGUN SIZE.
> Oshoosi!

OSHOOSI SIZE.
> Don't you get tired of going through this?
> Every morning we go through this.

OGUN SIZE.
> Nigga get yo' ass up!

OSHOOSI SIZE.
> This hard?
> Early in the morning you gotta be this hard?

OGUN SIZE.
> Man don't bring me that ...

OSHOOSI SIZE.
> That's your job.
> That car shop got your name, that's your job.

OGUN SIZE.
> Where your job?

OSHOOSI SIZE.
> I ain't got none.

I am currently seeking employment.
OGUN SIZE.
Currently?
OSHOOSI SIZE.
I'm tired!
OGUN SIZE.
So you just gone lay up here today?
OSHOOSI SIZE.
Yeah buddy.
I don't sleep good at night. and
tossed and turned all this morning.
Tired brother.
OGUN SIZE.
Kisses teeth
OSHOOSI SIZE.
Yeah man you should stay home
OGUN SIZE.
The shop man …
OSHOOSI SIZE.
Ogun you better stop man.
Stop doing it to yourself.
You keep working like that
Everyday all day at that damn shop
You gone work yourself to death man.
You better don't …
Death kill the lazy last.
OGUN SIZE.
Stop working?
OSHOOSI SIZE.
Nah … Rest.
Get you some ass.
OGUN SIZE.
Quit working?
OSHOOSI SIZE.
You own the car shop yeah?
That car shop yours.
Say Ogun's Carshack right?
OGUN SIZE.
Yeah …

OSHOOSI SIZE.

You ain't got to quit just get somebody to work it for you.

OGUN SIZE.

Deal.

OSHOOSI SIZE.

What?

OGUN SIZE.

You hired.

OSHOOSI SIZE.

Nigga!

OGUN SIZE.

You ain't got no job right …

OSHOOSI SIZE.

You know …

OGUN SIZE.

You "currently seeking employment … "

OSHOOSI SIZE.

Ogun …

OGUN SIZE.

Seek yo' ass into that truck in five minutes.

OSHOOSI SIZE.

I ain't applied for this job

I ain't even knowed you was hiring …

OGUN SIZE.

You more than qualified brother.

OSHOOSI SIZE.

Ah come on Og.

OGUN SIZE.

Effective today, Osi.

OSHOOSI SIZE.

Nah man, nah I'm turning this shit down.

I don't want your job.

OGUN SIZE.

Wait a minute …

OSHOOSI SIZE.

Oh shit …

OGUN SIZE.

You turning down work?

OSHOOSI SIZE.

Shit.

OGUN SIZE.

Oh man you turning down a lot of shit.

First off you forfeit your living here rights …

OSHOOSI SIZE.

You threatening me?

OGUN SIZE.

I promise you.

OSHOOSI SIZE.

Fuck that! I'll stay with Aunt Ele'!

OGUN SIZE.

Gua ain't gon put up with your shit!

Elegua ain't never like us and fo sure not you. You also forcing me to tell your parole officer

you won't work.

Smiles.

Ogun Size exits.

OSHOOSI SIZE.

Are you … Fo' real … This nigga!

OGUN SIZE.

From outside

Beep

OSHOOSI SIZE.

I swear fore god …

I swear this nigga …

Got the working love man. Shit.

Know a nigga don't feel like no

Getting up he come in here. "Oshoosi … " Like my name slave, Like my name on that damn car shop …

"Oshoosi"

That even … He like that shit,

Up all early in the morning working,

For what?

On what?

Nigga need to get up and build me a damn car. A nigga need to get around. How I'm supposed to get a girl,

Pick up, walk round on my feet?

Feet already flat

OGUN SIZE.

Beep!

OSHOOSI SIZE.
> You hold the hell on!
> Black bastard.
> If I am going to work I'ma smell G double O D good.
> Can't be workin and smelling like yo' ass ... Always funky.
> Nigga stay dirty!
> He ain't even that black.
> I was always darker than him.
> Everybody know that ...
> Damn shoe ...
> Everybody know I was darker 'cause of my daddy.
> His daddy was red.
> Redder than Mama.
> He walking around here ...

OGUN SIZE.
> Beep

OSHOOSI SIZE.
> Keep on Og!
> Keep on Ogun.
> Keep on the way you do.
> Every beep I'm a take even longer to get dressed.
> Going in there to get oil all on me n shit.
> You think I'm gone hurry up for that.
> That nigga threaten to tell my parole!
> He supposed to be my brother ...
> That ... He ...
> Boy I swear you can't win ...
> Not round here ...
> Huh!

OGUN SIZE.
> Coming back in, Osi!

OSHOOSI SIZE.
> Eh man ...

OGUN SIZE.
> Boy put that damn cologne down!

OSHOOSI SIZE.
> Look!

OGUN SIZE.
> Getcha ass in the car!

OSHOOSI SIZE.
    Laughing
    SomethingtomyselfcauseIdon'twantyoutohear'causeit'sforme
OGUN SIZE.
    Whatcha say? Say it again.
OSHOOSI SIZE.
    Mumbling man.
    I don't want to hurt your feelings.
OGUN SIZE.
    Huh.
    Ey!
    Don't slam my truck …
OSHOOSI SIZE.
    Outside.
    Slam!
OGUN SIZE.
    Bastard!

Scene 2

OSHOOSI SIZE.
    Oshoosi Size on lunch break,
    Drinking a Coke-cola
    Singing a song *(He sings.)*
ELEGBA.
    Elegba enters, drifting, like the moon …
    Sang that song nigga!
OSHOOSI SIZE.
    Huh? Ey 'Legba!
ELEGBA.
    You sing nigga and the angels stop humming …
OSHOOSI SIZE.
    You crazy.
ELEGBA.
    It's true, brother!
    Where you get a voice like that?
    I been wondering since lock-up,

14

"How Oshoosi get his voice?"

OSHOOSI SIZE.

Ah hell Legba you got a voice.

ELEGBA.

But my voice clear

I know that, I was born a choir boy.

But you? You a siren.

OSHOOSI SIZE.

What?

ELEGBA.

A siren! You ope up your mouth an' everybody know where
the pain at. Your voice come out and say, "the pain right here.
It's here, see it? See?"

OSHOOSI SIZE.

C'mon man …

ELEGBA.

You don't like nobody to brag on you …

OSHOOSI SIZE.

Nah man

ELEGBA.

That's alright I ain't scared to,

Everybody needs somebody to brag on him.

You like my brother man … I ain't scared to brag on you.

Ain't embarrassed about my brother.

Nah too cool to be embarrassed.

OSHOOSI SIZE.

My man 'Legba!

ELEGBA.

I see Og got you 'round here workin'.

OSHOOSI SIZE.

Lookin' like a grease monkey.

ELEGBA.

You shouldn'ta told him.

OSHOOSI SIZE.

Shit really, I didn't tell him.

ELEGBA.

Nah?

OSHOOSI SIZE.

Hell nah.

ELEGBA.

You didn't tell him that we worked on cars locked up?

OSHOOSI SIZE.

He ask what we do in the pen.

I say, "Wait, mutha … "

That's what we do.

Man sometimes he ask dumb ass questions.

He ask me what we do in the pen.

"Wait.

Cry.

Wait."

ELEGBA.

You right.

OSHOOSI SIZE.

I say, "Work and wait."

He say, "Work?"

I say, "Work …

Cry,

Shit,

Pray nigga.

What you think?"

ELEGBA.

What he say to that?

OSHOOSI SIZE.

And he look at me and say, "Work huh?"

ELEGBA.

That's it.

OSHOOSI SIZE.

I'm here.

ELEGBA.

You shouldn'ta told him everything.

OSHOOSI SIZE.

I spoke it all man.

ELEGBA.

You say it all?

All about the pen?

OSHOOSI SIZE.

ELEGBA.

OSHOOSI SIZE.

Nah I ain't tell him all that.

ELEGBA.

Yeah that shit ain't nothin.

OSHOOSI SIZE.

Nah. Hell nah.

The pen got me dreamin about pussy nightly.

ELEGBA.

Man …

OSHOOSI SIZE.

Had to hold your own self tight at night.

ELEGBA.

You didn't won't nobody to do it for you.

OSHOOSI SIZE.

Nah. Hell nah.

Niggas always offerin'.

ELEGBA.

Or trying to take it.

OSHOOSI SIZE.

That shit crazy, crazy shit.

I didn't think they would get like that.

ELEGBA.

Man when you in need your mind …

OSHOOSI SIZE.

Man …

Sometimes I had to remind myself

That I wouldn't gone be there that long.

ELEGBA.

Yeah you only had a year,

OSHOOSI SIZE.

Two.

ELEGBA.

Lucky nigga.

OSHOOSI SIZE.

Ah nigga you got out right after me.

ELEGBA.

Ey man, we went at the same time, came out same time.

We got close like that.

Helped each other.

OSHOOSI SIZE.

Yeah man.

ELEGBA.

We was like brothers.

OSHOOSI SIZE.

Yeah.

ELEGBA.

Brothers in need.

OGUN SIZE.

Ogun enters covered in oil!

ELEGBA.

Og!

OGUN SIZE.

Niggas!

OSHOOSI SIZE.

Why you got to be so hard all the time?

OGUN SIZE.

You need something 'Legba!

I didn't see no car?

ELEGBA.

Nah Og, just came to see my brother.

OGUN SIZE.

Where he at?

ELEGBA.

Ah, Size Number one, you know how we call each other brothers.

OGUN SIZE.

Pissed at being called Size Number one

Yeah I know how.

Osi, get that part I asked you for.

ELEGBA.

Well I guess I be going …

OSHOOSI SIZE.

Take it easy 'Legba.

ELEGBA.

Oh man you know …

OGUN SIZE.

Yeah you be easy 'Legba.

Bring a car next time you come through. Give me something to do while you brothers

Conversate …
ELEGBA.
Converse.
OGUN SIZE.
ELEGBA.
Elegba exits the way he came.
OSHOOSI SIZE.
Why you always got to …
OGUN SIZE.
I asked you for that part almost ten …
OSHOOSI SIZE.
Man I took a break.
OGUN SIZE.
Your ass couldn't've told me that
Before I was getting oil in my eyes!
OSHOOSI SIZE.
That's a good color on you.
OGUN SIZE.
Playin' thats what you always doin'.
OSHOOSI SIZE.
Man I was being cordial nigga.
OGUN SIZE.
You don't need to be nice to that nigga.
OSHOOSI SIZE.
That's my friend.
OGUN SIZE.
You don't make no friends in the pen.
OSHOOSI SIZE.
What you know?
OGUN SIZE.
Bring the part Osi.
OSHOOSI SIZE.
"Bring the part Osi."
ELEGBA.
Elegba returns
Ey …
OSHOOSI SIZE.
Oh you back man. I gotta get to work.
ELEGBA.
Nah, nah, I know.

But um listen.

You got a ride?

OSHOOSI SIZE.

Nah, not yet.

ELEGBA.

Your brotha the king a cars

And you ain't got no ride?

OSHOOSI SIZE.

Ain't that the shit?

ELEGBA.

You sayin' it man.

As much as you talked about getting a ride when we was

locked up …

OSHOOSI SIZE.

Yeah! Right.

ELEGBA.

All that talk about how riding is the ultimate freedom.

Every other word out yo' mouth was about a car …

Remember?

OSHOOSI SIZE.

I know …

ELEGBA.

Brother you talked about cars so much

I was scared for you to get out 'cause I swore

The first thing you was gone do was go out and steal you

one.

OSHOOSI SIZE.

Shut up Legba …

ELEGBA.

I'm just saying man …

Remember all you talk about was a car.

I say that nigga gone get him a car.

And you ain't got no car yet.

Man please how that work?

OSHOOSI SIZE.

I hear you 'Legba.

ELEGBA.

I'm just saying man.

You know me. I don't mean nothing.

Talk too much and too slow.

OSHOOSI SIZE.
> Nah you alright brother.
ELEGBA.
> Well I will let you get back
> I gotta get to work too.
OSHOOSI SIZE.
> You got a job nigga!
ELEGBA.
> Working at the funeral home.
OSHOOSI SIZE.
> Hell to the nah.
ELEGBA.
> Yeah it's paying good
> It's alright …
OSHOOSI SIZE.
> 'Legba man you working
> On dead people.
ELEGBA.
> Better than working with live people.
> This way nobody don't bother me.
OSHOOSI SIZE.
> I don't like the look of the dead.
ELEGBA.
> You gone be dead someday too.
OSHOOSI SIZE.
> Yeah but I don't need yo' ass to remind me.
ELEGBA.
> It's good to remember …
> So you know you need to do now
> So you know that you ain't got forever just right now.
> Good to remember death man.
OSHOOSI SIZE.
> I guess I hear you.
ELEGBA.
> Ey
> Osi man.
> I ain't mean to bring you down.
OSHOOSI SIZE.
> Nah man I'm alright …

ELEGBA.

Ey see about that car Oshoosi.

OSHOOSI SIZE.

Yeah. Yeah …

ELEGBA.

You my brother man.

OSHOOSI SIZE.

Ey man … I know that.

ELEGBA.

Lay it down …

Elegba offers his hand to Oshoosi.

OSHOOSI SIZE.

Oshoosi takes it, how could he not.

You alright man.

Scene 3

OGUN SIZE.

Ogun Size goes under the car.

OSHOOSI SIZE.

Ogun …

OGUN SIZE.

What?

OSHOOSI SIZE.

I need a ca …

OGUN SIZE.

Coming from under the car,

holding a part, irritated.

What?

OSHOOSI SIZE.

Um … What does that part do?

OGUN SIZE.

Sighs … Ignoring his baby brother.

I'm trying to concentrate!

Goes back under car

OSHOOSI SIZE.

How long you think before you retire?

OGUN SIZE.

I just started …

OSHOOSI SIZE.

Yeah but shit you doing good brother.

OGUN SIZE.

Huh.

OSHOOSI SIZE.

Hey Og …

OGUN SIZE.

Ogun comes from under the car.

Nigga they let you talk this much in the pen?

Ogun goes back under the car.

OSHOOSI SIZE.

Oshoosi kicks at his brother.

OGUN SIZE.

Ogun comes from under the car

OSHOOSI SIZE.

Oshoosi smiles innocently.

OGUN SIZE.

Ogun goes back under the car.

OSHOOSI SIZE.

OGUN SIZE.

OSHOOSI SIZE.

OGUN SIZE.

OSHOOSI SIZE.

Man I need some pussy.

OGUN SIZE.

Bang.

Shit!

OSHOOSI SIZE.

And the way you running into shit you need some too.

When was the last time you had some good coochie?

OGUN SIZE.

Comes from the under the car.

Coo? Did you say coochie?

When was the last time you had some?

OSHOOSI SIZE.

Nigga you know the answer to that!

I ain't been out but a minute.

Shit, seen more you than I seen myself.

You know I ain't had nothing for a minute.

Man but when I do … Boy looka here. BLOCKA!

OGUN SIZE.

Looks at Oshoosi like

"What the fuck"

OSHOOSI SIZE.

BLOCKA! BLOCKA!

OSHOOSI SIZE.

Shakes his head.

OSHOOSI SIZE.

OGUN SIZE.

Ogun goes back under the car.

OSHOOSI SIZE.

BLOCKA!

Ey Og …

Og whatever happened to Oya?

Huh. That girl had a thing for you.

Man she had a thing for you.

She loved her some Ogun Size.

In school I remember, you was in high school

And we go to the meets and she blow you a kiss while she

burning it up on that track.

She was so phyne, black as night, almost black as that asphalt;

all that ass!

All them legs like a Clydesdale legs. Sweet girl, Oya. Run like

the wind.

Whatever happened to her?

OGUN SIZE.

She was wit' my boy Shango.

She stop talking to me … started seeing him.

OSHOOSI SIZE.

Oh.

Man I'm

Sorry, I didn't know, that's fucked up …

OGUN SIZE.

Yeah. Yeah.

You know him right? Basketball team.

Go through women like draws … He in the army now.

Shango, my best friend … Huh.

He say to Oya, he walk to her one day, he say, "You should be with me.

Ogun ain't going nowhere. You should be with me."

Guess it sound sweet to her.

She start seeing him, talking to him. But he got other girls he seeing …

He come into town for furlough or whatever and he come to see 'em one by one.

He pay Oya some attention sometimes … See her sometimes I used to see her walking around, got this sad ass look on her face … like she sick.

She ain't sick just sad.

Sad like that after rain breeze … just sad.

I wanna grab her, sometimes, when I would see her,

I wanna grab and hold her so bad.

But she ain't mine no more.

She with that nigga … She with him.

I ain't say nothing … just respect that that's that man's girl.

She grown she in her own situation. You know … She …

Shango had this other girl … Guess it's his main girl.

Shun … She … man she beautiful … Shun. Beautiful.

All the niggas I know want her …

OSHOOSI SIZE.

Yeah I know Shun

BOTH.

Evil bitch …

OGUN SIZE.

She ain't neva been wrong to me. Always say hey Ogun how you doin. But she got that way about her. You know how she smiling but you know she think you beneath her. One of them kind. So she tells Oya she pregnant with Shango's baby. Just walked up to Oya with them hips you know and was like my name Shun, I got his baby so you ain't shit to him. And see Oya can't have no kids. Everybody know that. Now she scared she gone lose Shango. Which would be good if she left

the nigga … But she can't see that, nah she got to show him
how much she willing to do for Shango. How far she willing
to go for Shango. So she can't give him no child, she cut off
her ear.

OSHOOSI SIZE.

What!

OGUN SIZE.

Put it in a bowl and walked it to him while he was watching
TV at her house. She ain' scream uh nothing … Cut off her
ear and gave it to him. Say, I don't want nobody but you. Say
this mark me as yours … Nobody else want me they see this.
Shango left her ass there bleeding. Call her a crazy bitch, say
she sick. She wasn't sick … just sad. Sad.

She sitting like a lake up in the home they put her in …
laying on her back holding her head staring at the sky. You
look at her you, you think she floating somewhere. Oya.
Beautiful fast Oya. Sad girl.

OSHOOSI SIZE.

Man that's some van Gogh shit right there.

OGUN SIZE.

OSHOOSI SIZE.

OGUN SIZE.

What you know?

OSHOOSI SIZE.

What I …

OGUN SIZE.

Can't talk to you 'bout shit.

OSHOOSI SIZE.

What I say?

OGUN SIZE.

Nothing, just being you, nothing.
Nigga been outta jail all of five minutes
Think he know all.

Ogun goes back under the car.

26

Scene 4

OGUN SIZE.
Dinner unusually quiet
Eating.
OSHOOSI SIZE.
Eating
OGUN SIZE.
What you up to?
OSHOOSI SIZE.
Eaten my dinner …
OGUN SIZE.
I wanna know now, Os.
OSHOOSI SIZE.
Nigga?
OGUN SIZE.
Tell me …
OSHOOSI SIZE.
What's wrong wit' you?
OGUN SIZE.
You ain't never this quiet,
OSHOOSI SIZE.
I'm hungry … I'm tired …
OGUN SIZE.   .
Hungry?
You eatin' leftovers!
OSHOOSI SIZE.
Ey, I ain't ingratful …
OGUN SIZE.
That's the point you are.
You don't do nothing quiet;
You snore loud as hell,
You moan when you piss
And when you eat you talk more
Shit then you chew!
You up to something I don't know what it is
Oshoo but you better tell me now.

'Cause if I find out you doing some …
OSHOOSI SIZE.
Damn, boy I swear …
OGUN SIZE.
I'm not gone run to your rescue …
OSHOOSI SIZE.
Can't have no peace.
OGUN SIZE.
You think, "Ogun gone get me outta this"
You can forget that shit …
Don't do something to put your ass back in the pen!
OSHOOSI SIZE.
What?
OGUN SIZE.
I said …
OSHOOSI SIZE.
Ey man you want to go to jail Og?
Tell me, let me know I am sure I can arrange something.
'Cause you mention that shit 'bout every five fucking minutes …
I been home but two, three months …
In that time I swear you ain't let me forget once that I, at one time, was not free …
Why you got to be so hard all the goddamn time?
I'm the one who should be walking around like a stone man …
You act like you in jail …
You in jail Og? Hmm…?
Something holding you down Ogun?
If that's it you need to lose that shit and run man …
Before you become rock.
I ain't doin' nothing …
Just trying to live easy man …
Damn … it's gone be like this?
Let me know …
Let me know now 'cause I will get my shit,
Get my shit and go …
But while I am here …
Man you let me be free …
I got enough memories to wash out without you Putting in a

fresh supply every five minutes …
That shit ain't right …
It ain't right man …
It ain't.
OGUN SIZE.

OSHOOSI SIZE.

OGUN SIZE.

OSHOOSI SIZE.

OGUN SIZE.

OSHOOSI SIZE.
Goes back to eating
Eating
OGUN SIZE.

OSHOOSI SIZE.
Eating
OSHOOSI SIZE.
Ey man I need a ride …
OGUN SIZE.
I knew it!
Knew you were …
OSHOOSI SIZE.
Nigga you the king of cars …
OGUN SIZE.
You lookin around here?
I ain't the king of shit.
Kings don't come home greased from
The knees down.
OSHOOSI SIZE.
Ey, every man's castle ain't in England man.
Every man's palace ain't made of sand
And gold and shit.
Your palace made out of them cars Og.
You put cars back together better than any nigga 'cross this
place.

You the regent to come to about a car.

OGUN SIZE.

What you need a car for?

You ain't got no job to go to.

OSHOOSI SIZE.

That ain't what I'm talking about.

You know what I am talking about?

You pushing the conversation somewhere else!

We talking about cars, man.

I need a ride.

I want to drive somewhere …

OGUN SIZE.

Where? Yo' ass still on probation.

OSHOOSI SIZE.

Damnit son of a bitch!

OGUN SIZE.

Watch your mouth.

OSHOOSI SIZE.

I know I am still on probation!

I know Og.

Damn!

I know I was once in prison.

I am out and I am on probation.

Damnit man.

I ain't trying to drive to Fort Knox?

I ain't about to scale the capital …

I want a ride.

I want to drive out to the bayou …

Maybe take a lady down there …

And relax …

Shit what if I just wanted to go by myself?

What if I wanted to be there alone?

What difference it make?

Damn.

You can't fathom that?

You can't fit that round yo' big ass head?

You trying to lock me up again?

You trying to make my feet stuck?

Stuck here in here …

Well you just give me the word Og.

Tell me now like a man you want me to be miserable.
Fuck the car …
Mention prison again …
Make mention of it like you do …
That shit stops now.
I mean that.
I done served my time Ogun.
Sentence complete.
Done.
Done.
You sleep good tonight.
I won't.

Scene 5

OSHOOSI SIZE.
    Oshoosi Size is sleeping, that night, dreaming.
    And in his dream is his brother Ogun.
    Oshoosi can hear him, in this dream, working
    On something, on what?
OGUN SIZE.
    Huh!
OSHOOSI SIZE.
    Oshoosi is sleeping dreaming.
    Dreaming a sad dream and in his dream, enters
    Elegba too.
    Singing a sweet song.
ELEGBA.
    Mmm hmm.
OGUN SIZE.
    Huh
ELEGBA.
    Mmm hmm.
OGUN SIZE.
    Huh
ELEGBA.
    Oshoosi Size.

OGUN SIZE.
    Huh
ELEGBA.
    Cell number …
OGUN SIZE.
    Huh
ELEGBA.
    Inmate number.
OGUN SIZE.
    Huh
ELEGBA.
    Oshoosi
    Oshoosi Size.
    You remember?
    Don't you?
    Those late nights …
OGUN SIZE.
    Huh
ELEGBA.
    So hot.
OSHOOSI SIZE.
    So hot.
ELEGBA.
    When the walls come closer
    Closer …
    At night.
    Night …
OGUN SIZE.
    Huh
ELEGBA.
    Deep night …
    That's when it most dangerous …
    'Cause sometimes in the night …
OSHOOSI SIZE.
    Night.
OGUN SIZE.
    Huh
ELEGBA.
    You don't know what come for you, *wei?*

OGUN SIZE.

Huh

ELEGBA.

You know not where the hand will lead you.

OGUN SIZE.

Huh

ELEGBA.

If it's the good guard lead you back to your cell …

OGUN SIZE.

Huh

ELEGBA.

If it ain't …

OGUN SIZE.

Huh

ELEGBA.

You remember?

Me your friend …

Like your brother?

OGUN SIZE.

Huh

ELEGBA.

You brother in need.

I remember you … In there with me.

We were down in their sleep walking together.

Got so I could tell when you wanted to eat without

You saying it … tell when you wanted to piss or sleep

Or …

OGUN SIZE.

Huh

OSHOOSI SIZE.

Mmm.

ELEGBA.

I know you scared …

OSHOOSI SIZE.

Scared

ELEGBA.

I know you in that place.

OGUN SIZE.

Huh

ELEGBA.

Prison make grown men scared of the dark again.
Put back the boogie monsters and the voodoo man
We spend our whole life trying to forget …

OGUN SIZE.

Huh

ELEGBA.

You scared

OSHOOSI SIZE.

Scared …

ELEGBA.

I know you are …

OGUN SIZE.

Huh

OSHOOSI SIZE.

Dark.

ELEGBA.

But I am here in the dark …
I come for you like I always do …

OGUN SIZE.

Huh

ELEGBA.

In that night hour when you know nobody else
Around … 'Legba come down and sing for you …

OGUN SIZE.

Huh

ELEGBA.

You sing with me?
Mmm

OSHOOSI SIZE.

Mmm.

ELEGBA.

Yeah we sing so we know we together …

OGUN SIZE.

Huh

ELEGBA.

You and me make it so our harmony make a light …

OGUN SIZE.

Huh

ELEGBA.
>Light on the earth and the air …
>You and me
OGUN SIZE.
>Huh
ELEGBA.
>In the dark.
>I know you in that dark place …
>Where no one else knows you.
>You don't have to be scared no more …
OSHOOSI SIZE.
>*Mmm*
ELEGBA.
>*Mmm*
ELEGBA and OSHOOSI SIZE.
>*Mmm*
ELEGBA.
>Don't cry.
>Don't cry …
>I will walk you through
>Take you lightly into the night.
>Make you smile.
>Open your hand and smile.
>That M & M kind of smile.
OSHOOSI SIZE.
>Hah.
ELEGBA.
>It's funny ain't it Osi …
>Huh.
>Funny.
>Oshoosi Size …
>My brother …
>Can you walk with me?
>I am your taker.
>I am here to take you home.
>Just when you thought you walked alone.
>I am here.
OGUN SIZE.
>Osi …

ELEGBA.
    Here.
OGUN SIZE.
    Osi.
ELEGBA.
    Here.
OGUN SIZE and ELEGBA.
    Osi!

Scene 6

OSHOOSI SIZE.
    Oshoosi Size wakes from a nightmare.
    Realizing, ah hell, he late for work.

Scene 7

OSHOOSI SIZE.
    Oshoosi Size begins walking to work!
OGUN SIZE.
    STEP!
ELEGBA.
    STEP!
OGUN SIZE.
    Step
ELEGBA.
    Step
OSHOOSI SIZE.
    Hot sun on my back
    Hot in my face!
    Hot.
ELEGBA.
    Step

OGUN SIZE.
Step
ELEGBA.
Step
OGUN SIZE.
Step
OSHOOSI SIZE.
Making me walk
Through this hot ass sun!
Man!
OGUN SIZE.
Step
ELEGBA.
Step
OGUN SIZE.
Step
ELEGBA.
Step on
OSHOOSI SIZE.
He …
You know he can be …
He better be …
ELEGBA.
Step on
OGUN SIZE.
Just step on
OSHOOSI SIZE.
Why he left though?
He act like I wouldn't
Jus' gone go back to bed.
Just lay my ass down …
ELEGBA.
Step
OGUN SIZE.
Step on …
OSHOOSI SIZE.
I would've …
Sure as hell should've …
Laid my black ass right back down …
Left my damn keys in the house.

Door locked.
Now I got to …
This sun!
Fucking car shop.
Walking.
Ogun!
ELEGBA.
Step on
OGUN SIZE and ELEGBA.
Just step on.
OSHOOSI SIZE.
Nigga.
You wait til I see Ogun Henri Size!
I'm ah …
Boy!
I standing my ground today.
I'm cutting ties this afternoon.
I swear that.
Step.
OGUN SIZE.
Step
ELEGBA.
Step
OGUN SIZE.
Step on
ELEGBA.
Step on
OGUN SIZE.
Just step on
ELEGBA.
Step
OSHOOSI SIZE.
Well it's hard
ELEGBA.
It's hard,
OSHOOSI SIZE.
Lord almighty.
OGUN SIZE.
Step

OSHOOSI SIZE.
It's hard,
ELEGBA.
It's hard
OSHOOSI SIZE.
Lord almighty,
ELEGBA.
Mighty
OGUN SIZE.
Step
OSHOOSI SIZE.
Say it's hard
ELEGBA.
It's hard
OSHOOSI SIZE.
Lord almighty!
OGUN SIZE.
Step
OSHOOSI SIZE.
Come On Lord
ELEGBA.
A wella.
OSHOOSI SIZE.
Well I ain't been to Georgy Georgy …
ELEGBA.
Well
OSHOOSI SIZE.
But I been told
ELEGBA.
A wella
OSHOOSI SIZE.
I ain't been to Georgy Georgy.
ELEGBA.
Well
OSHOOSI SIZE.
But I been told
ELEGBA.
A wella
OSHOOSI SIZE.
That them sweet Georgia girls

OGUN SIZE and ELEGBA and OSHOOSISIZE.
Lord Amighty
OSHOOSI SIZE.
They make a man wanna die
ELEGBA.
A wella.
OSHOOSI SIZE.
Well it's hard ...
ELEGBA.
It's hard
OSHOOSI SIZE.
Lord Amighty
OGUN SIZE.
Step.
OSHOOSI SIZE.
It's hard.
ELEGBA.
It's hard.
OSHOOSI SIZE.
Lord Almight mighty.
OGUN SIZE.
Step.
OSHOOSI SIZE.
It's hard.
ELEGBA.
It's hard.
OSHOOSI SIZE.
Lord Amighty.
OGUN SIZE and ELEGBA and OSHOOSI SIZE.
Come on boys a wella.

Scene 8

OSHOOSI SIZE.
    Oshoosi at the shop!
    Standing breathing hard
    from the walk.
OGUN SIZE.
    Glad you could make it
OSHOOSI SIZE.
OGUN SIZE.
    Can you bring a box from the …
OSHOOSI SIZE.
    Stares at his brother …
OGUN SIZE.
    You here now no need to be …
OSHOOSI SIZE.
    You left me.
OGUN SIZE.
    You overslept.
OSHOOSI SIZE.
    You wake me up every morning …
OGUN SIZE.
    You …
OSHOOSI SIZE.
    You left me there …
    I ain't come here to work.
    I quit.
OGUN SIZE.
    You fired.
OSHOOSI SIZE.
    All the better.
    I will pack my shit.
OGUN SIZE.
    You don't have to leave.
OSHOOSI SIZE.
    I don't want to hear your shit Og you know.
    I don't.

41

OGUN SIZE.

You can stay.

Just find a job.

OSHOOSI SIZE.

I planned to.

OGUN SIZE.

Then we square brother.

OSHOOSI SIZE.

You left me.

OGUN SIZE.

I know.

OSHOOSI SIZE.

That's fucked up.

OGUN SIZE.

Huh.

You don't want me to treat you like you locked up no mo'.

What you say last night Osi?

You say don't tell me when to and what to do no more.

I listen.

I'm listening …

OSHOOSI SIZE.

You left me.

OGUN SIZE.

So you got to get up when you get up.

OSHOOSI SIZE.

Interrupts

I looked around and you was gone.

OGUN SIZE.

Not when nobody else tell you.

OSHOOSI SIZE.

I walked here …

OGUN SIZE.

You can't get up lessen you want to, no way.

OSHOOSI SIZE.

It was hot.

OGUN SIZE.

I can't get up for you.

OSHOOSI SIZE.

I'll see you at the house.

OGUN SIZE.

Yeah Realizing … You walked?

ELEGBA.

Elegba enters

ELEGBA and OSHOOSI SIZE.

Hell Yeah!

OSHOOSI SIZE.

Hot as hell out there.

ELEGBA.

Breathing hard …

OSHOOSI SIZE.

What's up 'Legba?

ELEGBA.

I had to push her here …

OGUN SIZE.

Push who?

Who you pushed?

ELEGBA.

I had to push her most of the way …

She wouldn't go up on me …

OGUN SIZE.

What you talking about?

OSHOOSI SIZE.

A realization

A car.

ELEGBA.

A car.

OGUN SIZE.

A car?

Where?

ELEGBA.

She down there.

A couldn't get her up that hill.

OSHOOSI SIZE.

Hell I barely made it up that hill.

OGUN SIZE.

But you made it.

ELEGBA.

Me and no car wasn't gone make it.

OSHOOSI SIZE.

Excited as hell!

A car!

ELEGBA.

Can you look at her Og?

OGUN SIZE.

You got money?

OSHOOSI SIZE.

Ey!

OGUN SIZE.

What?

ELEGBA.

I can pay you tell me what's wrong.

OGUN SIZE.

Down the hill?

Will it start?

ELEGBA.

Yeah.

OGUN SIZE.

Ogun exits

OSHOOSI SIZE.

Sorry about that.

ELEGBA.

What?

OSHOOSI SIZE.

Him, man, he can be hard sometimes.

ELEGBA.

It's alright.

You got a car?

OSHOOSI SIZE.

Nah.

ELEGBA.

Take this one.

OSHOOSI SIZE.

What you mean man?

ELEGBA.

OSHOOSI SIZE.

What you doing?

ELEGBA.

Nothing!

OSHOOSI SIZE.

Why you giving me a car?

ELEGBA.

Well I ain't giving it to you …

OSHOOSI SIZE.

Where it come from?

ELEGBA.

I found it.

OSHOOSI SIZE.

Nigga!

C'mon, 'Legba you found a car?

ELEGBA.

In my cousin's dump.

OSHOOSI SIZE.

What I'ma do with a car that don't work?

OGUN SIZE.

Excited breathing heavy

It's fine …

ELEGBA.

It's fine …

OSHOOSI SIZE.

It's fine?

OGUN SIZE.

Better then fine.

That car in good shape.

The outside beat up …

But even that's a cool blue

All you got to do is polish that up. You ain't have no problems
with cars like that …

Yeah you got to tune it up sometimes …

Pop it when it's buckin on you

But those one of those American classics.

Those, "I will run longer and stronger then the human body"
cars. Man please that car got plenty run in it.

OSHOOSI SIZE.

Why Legba couldn't get her to run?

ELEGBA.

I ain't got no license.

OSHOOSI SIZE.

Nigga you don't know how to drive?

ELEGBA.

I mean I do.

I think I do still remember.

But my license still suspended. Gotta get a new one.

Beside I ran into the Law the other day.

OSHOOSI SIZE.

Oh shit.

OGUN SIZE.

Ah nah.

ELEGBA.

Yeah.

OSHOOSI SIZE.

What he say?

OGUN SIZE.

He say something to you?

ELEGBA.

What he always say?

ALL THREE.

"Eh boy.

OGUN SIZE.

"What you doing 'round here?"

OSHOOSI SIZE.

"Stay out of the shit 'fore you start to stink."

ELEGBA.

"What you doing?

Where you going?

Better be quick."

OGUN SIZE.

I swear that man ain't neva gone change.

OSHOOSI SIZE.

Anytime he see another black man in

Town he act like he got to chase him out.

ELEGBA.

Sherriff act like he the only nigga

Can be seen in the town.

OSHOOSI SIZE.

He ask you questions too Og?

OGUN SIZE.

Man you know he treat everybody like

We guilty 'til proven innocent.

ELEGBA.
>	'Cept them white folks.
OSHOOSI SIZE.
>	Nothing but, "How do sir."
OGUN SIZE.
>	"Morning."
ELEGBA.
>	"Morning sir.
>	Y'all might want take shed of this sun lessen
>	You want to get as dark as me today.
>	Ha ha ha!"
OSHOOSI SIZE.
>	And they laugh too.
ELEGBA.
>	Yeah they do.
OGUN SIZE.
>	Laugh with the darkie play sheriff.
OSHOOSI SIZE.
>	Laugh nigga laugh.
OGUN SIZE.
>	"Lessen you want to get as dark as me."
ELEGBA.
>	He see me see him.
OSHOOSI SIZE.
>	Huh?
ELEGBA.
>	He see me look his way on the way to the Food Lion.
>	He look over his glasses.
OGUN SIZE.
>	That smile just coming off his face I bet.
ELEGBA.
>	The white people he talking to walk on by,
>	Some of the Witt boys.
>	They walk on by …
>	But he stay there looking at me.
OSHOOSI SIZE.
>	He had you in sights.
OGUN SIZE.
>	You caught him playing monkey.

OSHOOSI SIZE.

That's a crime in itself.

OGUN SIZE.

Punishable by death.

ELEGBA.

He say where you going 'Legba.

OSHOOSI SIZE.

He remember your name?

OGUN SIZE.

He call me Size.

OSHOOSI SIZE.

Call me Size too.

OGUN SIZE.

Like we twins …

OSHOOSI SIZE.

Or the same person.

OGUN SIZE.

Like it's only one of us.

OSHOOSI SIZE.

Like we the same.

ELEGBA.

"Where you going 'Legba."

"Nowhere sir."

Huh.

OSHOOSI SIZE.

Huh.

OGUN SIZE.

Huh.

ELEGBA.

"When they let you out?"

OSHOOSI SIZE.

Let you?

ELEGBA.

"They didn't let me do nothing.

I served my time.

Did all of it.

Got a job work at the funeral home."

OGUN SIZE.

'Legba you work at the …

OSHOOSI SIZE.

Leave it 'lone Ogun.

ELEGBA.

"You got you a job huh boy.

You think you fully rehabitulated son?"

OGUN SIZE.

What?

ELEGBA.

You know rehabitulated.

OSHOOSI SIZE.

What the fuck is that?

ELEGBA.

Ha, the nigga trying to say Rehabilitated.

OSHOOSI SIZE.

Niggas.

OGUN SIZE.

Stupid Nigga.

ELEGBA.

"You fully rehabitulated?"

"Yes sir I think I am."

"You think?"

"I think sir."

"You should know shouldn't you?"

"I guess."

"There you go again son, guessing, thinking …

That's what got you in trouble in the first place, ain't it?

Thinking you was too fast.

Thinking you could get away …

If you was better, you would know better than to

Think or guess ever again."

OSHOOSI SIZE.

What you say 'Legba?

OGUN SIZE.

What you say?

ELEGBA.

I say, "Maybe you right sir."

"Maybe!"

OGUN SIZE.

Oh no.

OSHOOSI SIZE.

Shit Legba.

ELEGBA.

"Maybe I'm right huh?

Well let's go see your parole officer see if he think

I'm right."

"What fo?"

"Well you bout to go back in ain't you?"

"Why!"

"You standing here loitering."

"No sir."

"You ain't, no?

Well you got a clear answer to that."

"Yes sir."

"Don't let me catch you running 'Legba."

"Sir?"

"Don't stand still and don't run …

Don't wanna see you riding or flying …

Every time I see you I better see you

Getting where you need to go,

Where you should be going,

The way God intended for you to get there,

Before the modern inventions of life made it

Easier for the scum of the earth to transport they evil deeds.

Back when all you had was your feet to the earth …

Don't let your transgressions vine up around you son … "

OSHOOSI SIZE.

"Don't let the weeds of the world strangle you."

OGUN SIZE.

"The mud … "

ELEGBA.

"Don't let it stick you and choke you.

Don't play in the shit you'll start to stink."

"Yes sir."

OSHOOSI SIZE.

"Yes sir."

OGUN SIZE.

Huh.

ELEGBA.

That's when the Witt boys came back.

Asked him if they could have a ride half back to the house.
They say they taken his advice trying not to catch sunstroke
Walking back home.
"You good boys come on catch a ride."
Smiling.
OSHOOSI SIZE.
    Beaming huh.
OGUN SIZE.
    Big smile.
ELEGBA.
    That M & M kind of smile.
OSHOOSI SIZE.
    Oshoosi stares at Elegba
    Like someone who just heard
    a ghost or remembered a dream.
ELEGBA.
    You know, like they just asked to blow sunshine up his ass.
OGUN SIZE.
    Might do.
OSHOOSI SIZE.
    Huh.
ELEGBA.
    So I decided to push her over rather than risk getting caught
    riding.
OSHOOSI SIZE.
    Nigga you crazy.
ELEGBA.
    How much you want for looking at her Size number one?
OGUN SIZE.
    Nothing man. It's cool.
ELEGBA.
    Ey thanks Ogun man that's nice of you.
OSHOOSI SIZE.
    Yeah man.
OGUN SIZE.
    Yeah well enjoy your car 'Legba.
    Get somebody teach you how to drive it.
    Don't see how you can with the Law pressin you …
ELEGBA.
    It ain't mine.

OGUN SIZE.
    I thought you just said …
ELEGBA.
    I brought it here for Osi.
OGUN SIZE.   OSHOOSI SIZE.
    A car?   A car.
ELEGBA.
    Yeah. Man.
    Here.
    Here.

ACT TWO

Scene 1

Oshoosi Size and Elegba follow the action described by Ogun.

OGUN SIZE.
    A week later …
    Ogun Size is sleeping,
    dreaming.
OGUN SIZE.

OGUN SIZE.
    And in his dream
    is his brother Oshoosi
    and his friend Legba.
OSHOOSI SIZE.

ELEGBA.

OGUN SIZE.
    In this dream of Ogun's
    There is something strange happening.
    His brother Oshoosi and 'Legba
    are bound together.
    And they seem to want to part ways, to separate.
    But they can't.
OSHOOSI SIZE.

ELEGBA.

OGUN SIZE.
    They can't seem to get loose of one another,
OSHOOSI SIZE.

ELEGBA.

> For a moment
> In this dream of Ogun's
> It seems that Elegba has changed
> His heart.
> And now 'stead of trying to get away from
> Shoosi he staying with him,
> Doing everything he can to be next to him.
> And now Shoosi looking confused …

OSHOOSI SIZE.

ELEGBA.

OGUN SIZE.

> Not knowing what to do,
> Where to go, how to move,
> Just feeling trapped,
> Feeling caught up in 'Legba.
> Wanting to get shed of 'Legba
> But not knowing how.
> Ogun wants to tell his brother
> To call him …
> Call me Shoosi I will help you.
> But nothing comes out of his mouth
> And nothing changes.
> Ogun Size wants to fix this dream,
> Right this wrong,
> But it's too late.
> Ogun's dream ends
> And Elegba is dragging
> His brother Oshoosi along with him
> And there ain't nothing he can do about it!

Scene 2

OGUN SIZE.
  Ogun waking up
  OSI!
OSHOOSI SIZE.
  Coming in
  What?
OGUN SIZE.
  Oshoosi?
OSHOOSI SIZE.
  What you screaming for?
OGUN SIZE.
  Hey man, listen …
OSHOOSI SIZE.
  What's wrong Og?
  Man you sweatin'.
OGUN SIZE.
  Yeah I was just …
  Sleeping.
OSHOOSI SIZE.
  You sleeping that's some shit.
OGUN SIZE.
  It was a nap you know …
OSHOOSI SIZE.
  Naps for old folk Ogun.
  You getting old …
OGUN SIZE.
  Yeah I guess.
  I mean …
OSHOOSI SIZE.
  I'm just messing with you man.
  Ey man listen thank you for the car man.
OGUN SIZE.
  Well see that's …
  The thing … I mean I fixed it for you …

OSHOOSI SIZE.

I know, I know … I need a job. But I am looking and
I think the Food Lion is gone be my best bet.

OGUN SIZE.

That's …

OSHOOSI SIZE.

Man I damn sure don't want to …
But ey, wouldn't be called work if I wanted
To do it.

OGUN SIZE.

Lil brother …

OSHOOSI SIZE.

But you got a career in the cars man.
You love doin that?

OGUN SIZE.

Yeah I love fixing …

OSHOOSI SIZE.

I need to find something like that for myself.
That car look beautiful.
You seen it?
'Course you seen it you fixed it.

OGUN SIZE.

Like? You can …

OSHOOSI SIZE.

I was thinking about going to school.

OGUN SIZE.

Oh. Oh yeah?

OSHOOSI SIZE.

Yeah man take some classes take one of them aptitude tests or
something …
I took something like that in the pen …
You know it said something like I should work in social work.
I'm supposed to be sensitive to other people's needs and shit
…

OGUN SIZE.

Nigga …

OSHOOSI SIZE.

Ha I'm serious.
I just want to find something like you got …
But with lots of vacation time man …

56

I want to see so much.

So much …

See everything.

In the pen I would sit in the library …

OGUN SIZE.

Oshoosi …

OSHOOSI SIZE.

They had this one book was this big-ass book full of pictures of Madagascar. I mean just the people, the places, the water, the eating, the ground the earth, the fucking, fecundity!

OGUN SIZE.

Fe … Fecundity?

OSHOOSI SIZE.

You like that!

OGUN SIZE.

Ha, yeah!

OSHOOSI SIZE.

All these black-and-white and color pictures no words.

One of the reasons why I picked it up probably …

I'm a start reading more!

I ain't no idiot I mean I should read about this world …

I wanna go.

OGUN SIZE.

Osi.

OSHOOSI SIZE.

I want to go to Madagascar!

Hell I wanna go to Mexico man it's right there!

Right there and I ain't ever been.

OGUN SIZE.

What?

OSHOOSI SIZE.

You know what fucked me up Og?

This what got me man …

I am looking at this book and I am thinking wow this place look far away, far as hell … This place out there, these people ain't even got on no clothes hardly and then I see it.

OGUN SIZE.

What?

OSHOOSI SIZE.

This man …

This nigga ...

This man ...

He look just like me!

I swear somebody trying to fuck with me ...

'Legba or the warden don got a picture of me and stuck it in this book about Madagascar with me half naked 'n' shit ...

But it ain't!

Him and me could've been twins man!

He standing and you know what he saying ...

What it look like he saying?

"Come on lets go."

I can see it in his eyes!

I need to be out there looking for the me's.

He got something to tell me man.

Something about me that I don't know 'cause I am living here and all I see here are faces telling me what's wrong with me.

Maybe the me in China can tell me why I can't sleep at night.

Shit man who knows ...

Man!

Ha.

Ha.

I smoked too much today talking shit, right?

OGUN SIZE.

Nah man you ...

Wait you smoked?

OSHOOSI SIZE.

Yeah just a li'l bit ...

OGUN SIZE.

Osi!

OSHOOSI SIZE.

Don't worry about it.

The Food Lion don't give drug tests, besides it's weed ...

It ain't like I was shooting up or some dumb shit like that.

OGUN SIZE.

I know ...

OSHOOSI SIZE.

I'm doing good Og you don't got to worry about me.

Ey man your work ain't being done in vain man.

I love what you did to the ride man.

That shit is ... it's beautiful.

I love you for it.

I mean when you brought it home today I was like damn it man it look so good I don't want to touch it.

OGUN SIZE.

It's yours …

OSHOOSI SIZE.

I'm going be real careful in it.

OGUN SIZE.

Please …

OSHOOSI SIZE.

Yeah I know …

Me and 'Legba just going to the outlet …

Gone see what's playing at the pictures.

Mostly going to see the women that come out for the pictures.

I got enough for gas but not for the movie. Hell ain't nothing out really that I want to see.

Would like to see some thongs walk by.

And once they see me and 'Legba and that sparkling ride they wanna show me they panny line.

I am down for inspection.

ELEGBA.

From outside.

Beep

OGUN SIZE.

What the hell?

OSHOOSI SIZE.

That must be Legba out there fucking around.

OGUN SIZE.

Ey man …

OSHOOSI SIZE.

Laughing. To Elegba

Ey man!

Nigga

OGUN SIZE.

Osi …

OSHOOSI SIZE.

I got it Og.

ELEGBA.

Beep

59

OSHOOSI SIZE.
> Ha Ha!
> Ey nigga!
> Stop wearing out my horn I'm coming.
> They arrest nigga's just for that these days …
> Get your arm out my window.

OGUN SIZE.
> Osi.

OSHOOSI SIZE.
> Yeah Og?

ELEGBA.
> Beep.

OSHOOSI SIZE.
> Keep on crazy Kat.

OGUN SIZE.
> Ey.

OSHOOSI SIZE.
> I'm a be fine …
> Fo sho.
> Go back to sleep Og.
> Go 'head.
> Oshoosi exits.

Scene 3

ELEGBA.
> Elegba standing in the early morning air, outside
> At Oshoosi's Window.
> Oshoosi, calling …

Oshoosi Size.
> You hear me …
> I know you do …
> If you in there I know you hear what 'Legba say.

OGUN SIZE.
> Ogun Size enters,
> With his shovel …
> He sees Elegba at his Brother's window,

Deep breath

ELEGBA.
> Hey … Size Number One,
> How you doin?
> You up early this morning …

OGUN SIZE.
> Morning 'Legba …
> Oshoosi still sleep, man,
> You have to come back later on
> If you wanna talk.

ELEGBA.
> So he here …

OGUN SIZE.
> You need something?

ELEGBA.
> You saw him? He here?

OGUN SIZE.
> 'Legba …

ELEGBA.
> I just want to tell him something.

OGUN SIZE.
> What, it can't wait 'til …

ELEGBA.

OGUN SIZE.

ELEGBA.

OGUN SIZE.
> What you … What's happening 'Legba?

ELEGBA.

OGUN SIZE.
> What's wrong?
> Something wrong with my brother
> What's … You hear me talking to you nigga.

ELEGBA.
> Why you up so early?

OGUN SIZE.
> I'm always up this early!

ELEGBA.

You been working on that little piece of road

for a minute there

OGUN SIZE.

What you know about me!

That ain't no problem for you

Is it?

What you come to tell my brother?

ELEGBA.

Ask him.

OGUN SIZE.

How he know if you ain't told him yet?

ELEGBA.

He just ain't told you yet.

OGUN SIZE.

So you got riddles for me this day

'Legba.

ELEGBA.

You shouldn't be out here this early.

You should be sleeping or something ...

It's still night it's so early.

OGUN SIZE.

You got something to say to me say it.

ELEGBA.

I told you who I come for.

OGUN SIZE.

Well he in my house and I say he sleep.

ELEGBA.

Keep him there ... Locked up in your spot

Size Number One

'Cause if the law catch him ...

OGUN SIZE.

ELEGBA.

Go in the house Ogun.

It's too early for you to be out here.

You don't know who you run into this late at night,

This early in the morning.

Go in the house ...

OGUN SIZE.

I run into you 'Legba.

I run into you.

ELEGBA.

Go on building your way, Ogun

Go on … we ain't need to talk this morning.

You don't need to hear what 'Legba say.

OGUN SIZE.

Don't do me no favors 'Legba.

You hear me …

Don't hold nothing back that's

Gone beat me down later.

Gone head and say what you gone say.

ELEGBA.

How come you never like me Size number One?

OGUN SIZE.

'Legba you trying to pull some bullshit?

Hear me. You trying something else?

Now you got something going on

Let me find out what it is from you man.

'Cause I swear if I find out later and you

Could have told me when I see you

I'm put my foot through you clean!

ELEGBA.

OGUN SIZE.

ELEGBA.

One night we was in … we was locked up

He hadn't been in there that long

Hell I hadn't been in long …

But he just got there

And he was strong.

Quiet to hisself.

Singing to hisself always

Most beautiful man ever seen.

He … call for you …

One night he just say I want my brother

Somebody call my brother …

Crying it like a child scared of the boogie monster coming

This grown man this man,
Crying for his brother ...
Sobbing into the night,
"Og come for Shoosi now ...
Come on now."
And at first I thought oh hell they gone get him for that
They gone hurt him for being so soft
But nah, there was a wail in that call,
He call on you so hard,
Call for his brother like pastors call on Jesus,
Wanting for you like the sun wants to shine!
Can't do nothing but grieve for a man who miss his brother
like that
Sound like a bear trapped in some flesh tearing snare
hollering like that
Can't mock no man in that much earthly pain.
He cry out and hell he make us all miss our brothers, The
ones we ain't neva even have
All the jailhouse quiet,
The guards stop like a funeral coming down the halls
In respect, respect of this man mourning the loss of his
brother
and you just hear the clanging of that man voice
Bouncing on the cement and the steel ... chiming like a bell
'Til he calm down ... 'til he just whispering your name now ...
My brother ... my brother ... where my brother ...
Gurgling it up out from under the tears ...
My brother ...
OGUN SIZE.

ELEGBA.
I look down at my feet I say I got to meet him ...
That brother ... that brother that make a man get on his
knees and cry out for that brother! I say to myself I got to
meet him ... I need to meet this brother Ogun Size.
OGUN SIZE.
Sorry to disappoint you 'Legba
ELEGBA.
Nah nigga you ain't disappoint 'Legba, you surprise me but
you ain't disappoint me. See I ain't had no hope in you, I ain't

the one you disappoint when you don't come visit and you
don't write more than a few words for letters. No you ain't
disappoint me nah. I ain't the one.
OGUN SIZE.

ELEGBA.
I can't never be his brother like you his brother. Never. You
know that right. No need to hate 'Legba. I can't stop you
from being his brother.
OGUN SIZE.

ELEGBA.
The law might come 'round this morning.
He might come round here looking for a Size.
I ain't saying which one.
Not sure if he know which Size he want.
But seeing as how he ain't got you …
Must be another Size he want to try on.
Must be another Size he ain't catch up with yet.
Always a way to go.
Gone 'head to work Ogun.
Gone to your shop.
OGUN SIZE.

ELEGBA.
Go on.
OGUN SIZE.
Ogun exits to work.

Scene 4

OGUN SIZE.
Slam
Since day one …
Day one,
You been fucking up …
Not just the other day when you was standing here,
looking all lost and stupid; all high on life
And the little bit of weed that Food Lion won't find in your piss.
Nah hell nah.
FROM DAY ONE.
Aunt Elegua stopped taking us to church.
I stopped going cause I ain't want to go in the first place.
But you kept getting up in the morning, you kept getting up every Sabbath,
And going down to the river to wash your fucking sins away …
And everybody say, "Look at Little Size taking up the cross with Jesus."
"Look at him he only nine."
"Look at that devotion for Jesus!"
"You should do like your brother Ogun … You should go to church like Shoosi!"
You know what I wanted to say? "Fuck that nigga and the church."
I was jealous.
I was.
I have to admit that right here in your face, I say, "Why couldn't I be devoted like Oshoosi."
Why didn't I want to sit in the boring-ass church all day and listen to the hypocrites sing songs on high to a God that ain't listening? 'Cause he wasn't, He ain't, He wasn't then and He ain't now … I been praying for yo' ass like a fool and no God!
No God, just sun and work and fuck ups from you …
I wanted to be you for a moment, Little Size, I wanted to be just like my little brother until me and Elegua found you

using the money you was stealing from collection in a crap game.
Yeah. Yeah.
And then everything turned. Everything turned. Spun right round. Landed on me.
Everybody like, "He only nine."
"If you would have been a better role model for him Ogun he wouldn't acted like this,"
If I would've … If I … " But Aunt Elegua sealed it though … that miserable old-ass lady …
She made my whole world crash down in front of me … She say, "Your mama would have been so disappointed in you … Letting your brother go like that. Yemoja would have hated you failing her Ogun. Letting your brother go." Letting you go … I let you go? I let you go. Me. She said Mama name … she never say Mama name but she threw that shit in my face.
I got one image of my mama in my mind, one … and it fucks with me at night … You hear me, it's the shit that keep me up building a fucking driveway to Nowhere …
Shit that won't let you lay down right …
She standing near the water, my mama standing out looking out, looking out towards the Gulf, belly full of you and she standing there holding my hand.
Tight.
Tight.
Tight.
Just her and the water …
Us. That's all I got left of my mama, and you in that picture. You a part of all I got left nigga.
So when Aunt Elegua in all her wisdom decided to make my ass feel guilty about you, that thought, that thought … Spring up in my head … my mama holding my brother inside and me tight, gripping.
So I held on from that day …
I gripped onto your ass and pushed you through school … I forced you up and out …
Whatever the fuck you … I did it … I burned my chance at anything so that I didn't leave you behind … I would run after you and ahead of you always hoping that I could keep

my grip on you or at least catch you before anyone else did.
But no matter what I did ... No matter if I thought you were
fine ... I thought you were gonna be okay somehow you
would slip through and fuck up and fuck up and fuck up
and when you fucked up somehow I fucked up! Somehow
there is no escaping you! You say I ain't never been in the pen?
Nigga whenever you fall everyone look at me like I fucking
pushed you ... That's my fucking life sentence ... That's my
lockdown ... All my life I carry your sins on my back ...
And now you out there riding around in a car that I souped
up and popped off only so they could find you in it with a
fucking pound of powder! YEYO!
What the fuck?

OSHOOSI SIZE.

It wasn't mine Ogun ...

OGUN SIZE.

Shut up! Shut up, shut the fuck up.
You shut up don't say a fucking ... You fucked up ... Say
that! You wanna say something for once in your life say
something for me ... You fucked up, you fucked up, you
fucked up, you fucked up you fucked up you fucked up, you
fucked up you fucked up you fucked up you fucked up you
fucked up you fucked up you fucked up you fucked up you
fucked up. You fucked up!

OSHOOSI SIZE.

I.

OGUN SIZE.

You fucked up

OSHOOSI SIZE.

He ...

OGUN SIZE.

You fucked up

OSHOOSI SIZE.

I fucked up.

OGUN SIZE.

OSHOOSI SIZE.

OGUN SIZE.

So what you doin in here, hiding out?

OSHOOSI SIZE.

I don't need that shit from you …
You don't know what you talking about
I ain't did nothing.

OGUN SIZE.

That ain't what 'Legba say.
Hell that ain't what the law say.
The law, that's right.
He come to my door at the shop today and
Say he looking for the other Size.
I say what you talking about.
Say he looking for the other Size …
I say ain't but one Size here.
My heart sink down Shoosi …
My heart drop down I swear to God it did.
You was doing so good. So good.
Even when 'Legba say that you might be in trouble
I ain't believe. Wasn't till the law come up on me like that.

OSHOOSI SIZE.

I ain't did nothing!

OGUN SIZE.

What he lying?
Say he lying Shoosi?
Please, tell me how he …
If you convince me he lying I'm with you …
Tell me how he lying Oshoosi!
The law running around here …
Looking for you …
I … don't wanna know …
Yeah I do …
But … I …
You gotta …
You have to …
Please …
You have to … C'mon …

OSHOOSI SIZE.

'Legba and me was going to the outlet. He had a gym bag out
there said he had to spend the night near the bayou.

Said his cousin Nia was gone let him stay with her for a while out by the water.

I didn't know what the hell was in the bag. How the hell I know what he carrying? Man say he spending the night at his cousin.

I think he got clothes in the motherfucker.

The night was going good Ogun you know …

It was right …

We left the pictures, we look at the girls for a minute, few of 'em smiling … few of 'em laughing. But you know he want me to drive out there, wanted me to go out there … And drop him off.

So I say okay.

What laws I break?

Huh … Tell me …

I drove too fast out to Nia's. Yeah that I did do. 'Cause I remembered how phyne she use' to be … I wanted to see if I could get at her … See if I could lay there for a while … Blocka. Get that pussy. I had sin on my mind but not in my heart. So I was racing. And I'm just going and I got the wind coming in the car and the songs playing and 'Legba laughing, 'cause we having a good time … It's nice out … ain't too hot yet … And … and I'm driving and singing … *(He sings.)* … Just feel right that they played it, *(He sings.)* … I can feel Nia singing it to me you know. Inviting me to spend the night too. I'm singing and I caught a breeze right in my nose, that brackish water breeze right in my fucking nose and I sneezed … and the car spun right round. And I stopped and snot was hanging out my nose, I was laughing my ass off, it was so funny. 'Legba was laughing and it was dark and shit … It was real dark and laughing and then … And then

Felt like a fucking dream. Music still playing,

ELEGBA.

Elegba enters, singing

(He sings.)

Ogun stands watching,

OSHOOSI SIZE.

I felt like I had been there before.

ELEGBA.
(He sings.)
OSHOOSI SIZE.
> Just us out there … Just the car sitting and chillin' hearing
> that ole music … hearing it say something but really just
> telling me that I'm free and everything alright … 'Legba say,
> 'Legba say,

ELEGBA.
> This nice man.

OSHOOSI SIZE.
> I say yeah man.
> Yeah it is.
> He say let's …

ELEGBA.
> Let's just sit for a minute …

OSHOOSI SIZE.
> I say alright man
> but not too long gotta get to your cousin,

ELEGBA.
> Yeah but this nice, right?

OSHOOSI SIZE.
> He say this nice …
> I say yeah man you right. It was Ogun. I ain't gone lie. I never
> felt like that. Just sitting and being cool. I mean I just forgot
> life could be good sitting still. You try to tell me to be still but
> I ain't listen. Not til I near bout run off the side of the road I
> realize life can be sweet still. I smell that Gulf air. Just making
> me think more of Nia. Remember her body. How she walk
> like. Music making me sleepy.

ELEGBA.
(He sings.)
OSHOOSI SIZE.
> Making me sleepy and hard at the same time … Why that
> happen Ogun, why when you get sleepy yo' dick hard?
> Guess that mystery to be solved by scientist and astrologers
> or people who got plenty of time to study dick … All this a
> dream it was so quiet out there …

ELEGBA.
(He sings.)

ELEGBA and OSHOOSI SIZE.
(They sing.)
OSHOOSI SIZE.
(He sings.)
ELEGBA.

> Elegba touches Oshoosi head

OSHOOSI SIZE.

> It couldn't be happening.

ELEGBA.

> Let's, let's stay for a second.
> 'Legba's hand rests on Shoosi shoulder.

OSHOOSI SIZE.

> Not for real ...

ELEGBA.
(He sings.)

> His hand slides down ...

OSHOOSI SIZE.

> Not like that.

ELEGBA.
(He sings.)

> Slides down onto his thigh.

OSHOOSI SIZE.

> What you doin?

ELEGBA.

> Elegba smiling
> Nothing brother ...
> Just singing to you like I used to.
> This nice ain't it ...

OSHOOSI SIZE.

ELEGBA.

> Right?

OSHOOSI SIZE.

ELEGBA.
(He sings.)
OSHOOSI SIZE.

> And then I heard sirens.
> Come out nowhere lights and sirens.
> Music playing.

The Law come up on us looking like he happy 'bout
something.
Shining his light.
"You got anything in the trunk son"?
No sir. Nothing was in there as far as I know. Legba should've
spoke the fuck up. If he knew something was back there
shoulda said something. "No sir."
"Well what in shit is this?"
I hate how some niggas don't know how to cuss right.
Who say what in the shit?
"What in the shit is this?"
Huh … uh uh uh.
He standing holding this bag wide open.
He ain't supposed to search the car unless he got provocation
So he know he wrong but damnit if the sheriff ain't standing
there holding
'Legba's bag
And it's pouring white out onto the asphalt.
I be damned.
I wish you could've seen my face …
I wish you could've,
Hell I wish I coulda.
I like to jump over and kill 'Legba
But the law say get out the car.
I say, "'Legba what the fuck he holding man.
What you doing?"
He just looking.
Almost like he smiling.
I say tell him that shit ain't mine man.
He ain't say nothing.
Just stand there.
I say, "Say that shit ain't mine 'Legba."
He ain't say shit.
The Law walk back over to his car smiling his big-ass smile.
That "I got you" smile. That "cat caught mouse" smile.
Beaming from around his fat-ass head … Beaming.
I look at 'Legba and he still ain't saying shit …
He ain't doing shit.
And I see where he at already … I see where 'Legba at.
He in jail.

That's where …

He gone. He already sitting in his cell singing.

ELEGBA.

Come on and go with me …

OSHOOSI SIZE.

He back there just that fast.

ELEGBA.

Come on over to my place.

OSHOOSI SIZE.

And I see him go there …

I see them walls around him …

ELEGBA.

Come on and go with me …

OSHOOSI SIZE.

I see them dark-ass halls and the midnights with no sleep.

I swear I see 'em Ogun as you my brother I see 'em.

ELEGBA.

Come on over to my place.

OSHOOSI SIZE.

And I can't.

I just can't.

So I ran.

I can't tell you what I ran like, how I ran … what I saw when I ran …

I ran …

I run all the way 'til I get here.

And I come in here and I close the door and I say I ain't going back …

I ain't going back.

OGUN SIZE.

Ogun Size stares at his brother.

OSHOOSI SIZE.

Oshoosi Size his younger brother.

I am here now … Brother Size …

I'm here. What we gone do?

Scene 5

OGUN SIZE.
> That same night.

OSHOOSI SIZE.
> Later on.

OGUN SIZE.
> Laughing …

OSHOOSI SIZE.
> … His ass off
> I swear to God

OGUN SIZE.
> Nigga you lying!

OSHOOSI SIZE.
> You trying to tell me you ain't say it?

OGUN SIZE.
> I ain't neva said no shit like …

OSHOOSI SIZE.
> I remember it …
> I remember it like it was yesterday.
> Roon had just came 'round the house and told us that Mama
> finally passed
> Finally came over to the house …
> I was little but I wasn't that damn little.
> Roon came over there and told Aunt Elegua, "She gone Ele."
> That's how he say it … He say, "She gone Ele. Yemoja finally
> let go." I never did know what that meant "finally" …
> I mean. I know now …
> Anyway Roon turn around and see us standing there and
> walk over to us.
> And he said li'l men yo' mama ain't coming here to get
> you.
> She went to be a part of the number.
> She went on with the father now.
> Y'all don't be sad or scared.
> Yo' mama ain't coming. He say, you understand li'l man?
> Getting all close in my face breath smelling like snuff …

75

All Loud.
YOU UNDERSTAND LI'L MAN?
I say yeah I hear you.
Anything to get yo' ass out my face.
I gotcha.
He look at you he say you be strong Ogun
And I swear you could see the tremor start in your face …
OGUN SIZE.
Hahah!
Shut up …
OSHOOSI SIZE.
Like the Mississippi swelling up.
You so ugly when you cry.
If you cried today I still bet it's ugly …
You say
OGUN SIZE.
Go on now.
OSHOOSI SIZE.
You say,
"LORD GOD … WILL THIS PAIN … EVER GO AWAY!"
Knees buckled from under you.
Falling on the ground grabbing up the carpet underneath
you. Convulsing and weeping and wailing like Mary.
I like to cried 'cause I thought you was finna die.
I say Lord you done took my mama not my brother too.
OGUN SIZE.
Haha!
It ain't funny Oshoosi
I was in grief.
OSHOOSI SIZE.
You ass was overdramatic!
OGUN SIZE.
Hah!
OSHOOSI SIZE.
Then Aunt Ele kept calling you carpet boy for so long after.
OGUN SIZE.
That woman don't got a sympathetic bone her in body.
OSHOOSI SIZE.
But damn sure got a lotta body.

OGUN SIZE.

You ain't neva lied.

OSHOOSI SIZE.

Then gon have the nerve to have a fainting spell at Mama's
funeral. Fat ass …

OGUN SIZE.

Like somebody could hold her big ass up.

OSHOOSI SIZE.

Thank god for O Li Roon

Because I wasn't about to try and revive her nothing.

Her big ass passed out,

I say let her stay out that teach her ass for fainting.

I wasn't going nowhere near her.

OGUN SIZE.

Hateful Aunt Elegua.

OSHOOSI SIZE.

Sitting over there old as she wanna be.

Like she ain't never gone die.

Walking negro spiritual.

Just keep rolling along.

OGUN SIZE.

Seem like she never liked us,

Liked she resented Mama for getting sick

And having to take us in.

OSHOOSI SIZE.

Wasn't like we didn't come with two nice welfare checks

To go 'long with us.

Hell the government might as well put money clips 'round us
and handed us to her.

OGUN SIZE.

And she still gypped us at Christmas.

OSHOOSI SIZE.

Ain't that some shit?

Thank God for Santa Claus.

OGUN SIZE.

You believe in Santa?

OSHOOSI SIZE.

My big brother leaving me presents under the tree …

Yeah I believe.

OGUN SIZE.
   You knew it was me?
OSHOOSI SIZE.
   Who else it gone be?
   Nobody else care.
OGUN SIZE.

OSHOOSI SIZE.
   You act like you don't care …
   You act like you so tough but I would catch it …
   I catch you looking at me sometimes like you wanna beat my
   ass you so mad.
   Then I see this smile crack.
   I see it and I see you …
OGUN SIZE.

OSHOOSI SIZE.

OGUN SIZE.
   What you do in prison?
OSHOOSI SIZE.
   Man why you always ask that?
OGUN SIZE.
   You know what I do when you was gone …
OSHOOSI SIZE.

OGUN SIZE.
   Think about what you was doing right then.
   Try to see if I could think what you was doing in the pen.
   Sometimes a bad spell would hit me and my mind see
   terrible things happening to you. Fights and wonder how you
   sleeping.
   Sometimes I see you in there smiling big.
   That's one thing about you I do know …
   You kind to everybody.
   You give everybody a chance and yeah you fuck up but that's
   how the world balance you out.
   All that niceness you pass to everybody they take it and it
   comes back so that when you do fuck up you paying for it ain't
   so bad.

78

You good to everybody you meet.

I thought you come out of the pen hardcore, dark and mad as hell.

You came out same cool-ass Oshoosi, laid back laughing smiling thinking about pussy. Only thing prison made you was tired.

OSHOOSI SIZE.

You right Og, I'm tired man. So tired.

Tired. Too tired to fight it off.

OGUN SIZE.

Ogun Staring at his brother not knowing what to say

OSHOOSI SIZE.

Oshoosi looking at the ground thinking of all he done said …

OGUN SIZE.

Nothing more to say …

OSHOOSI SIZE.

Weary of saying anything

OGUN SIZE.

Weary of talking

OSHOOSI SIZE and OGUN SIZE.

Weary

OGUN SIZE.

(He sings.)

OSHOOSI SIZE.

Aw hell nah.

I'm already on the cusp of crazy you trying to push me over.

OGUN SIZE.

What?

OSHOOSI SIZE.

Nigga you know you can't sing.

OGUN SIZE.

Ey, the song just popped into my head.

OSHOOSI SIZE.

Pop it out.

OGUN SIZE.

Ey, I use to sing you to sleep.

OSHOOSI SIZE.

No I use to close my ears until I passed out.

OGUN SIZE.

Ha. You the singer.

OSHOOSI SIZE.

Nah man you crazy.

OGUN SIZE.

Sing that song for me I want to hear it.

OSHOOSI SIZE.

Nah c'mon Og.

OGUN SIZE.

You ain't sleeping no time soon.

Me neither.

Morning ain't for a while yet sing something man

I ain't heard you in a long time.

Not full out.

I mean I hear you in the shower.

But c'mon sing for me.

OSHOOSI SIZE.

OGUN SIZE.

OSHOOSI SIZE.

I tell you what ...

OGUN SIZE.

What?

OSHOOSI SIZE.

Play back up for me.

OGUN SIZE.

What!

OSHOOSI SIZE.

Don't act like you ain't never done it before.

OGUN SIZE.

Nigga ...

OSHOOSI SIZE.

Hold on ...

OGUN SIZE.

Where you going?

OSHOOSI SIZE.

Hold the hell on.

Coming.

I'll be right there.

Turns on music

OGUN SIZE.

That sweet song start playing.

I didn't know you had this song.

OSHOOSI SIZE.

Every man need a copy of this song.

OGUN SIZE.

Man you use' to sing the hell out of this song.

OSHOOSI SIZE.

Still do.

But I need a piano man.

OGUN SIZE.

You mean a organ man.

OSHOOSI SIZE.

Ah nigga just play whatever but in the back.

OGUN SIZE.

Alright Ike I'm getting.

OSHOOSI SIZE.

(Singing with the music …)

OGUN SIZE.

I think I'm a switch to drums.

OSHOOSI SIZE.

Good work brother.

OGUN SIZE.

I thought you would enjoy that brother.

C'mon sing the song.

OSHOOSI SIZE.

(Singing.)

OGUN SIZE.

Yeah!

OSHOOSI SIZE.

(Singing.)

OGUN SIZE.

What you got do?

OSHOOSI SIZE.

(Singing.)

OGUN SIZE and OSHOOSI SIZE.

(Singing at the same time.)

OSHOOSI SIZE.

Laughing

Eh you kinda over stepping your boundaries piano/sax man.

OGUN SIZE.

Having a good time …

Eh man I am just backing you up.

Just sing the song Anna Mae.

OSHOOSI SIZE.

(Singing.)

OGUN SIZE.

Now you getting into it!

But don't turn into a Temptation.

Keep it cool.

OSHOOSI SIZE.

Let me do this!

OGUN SIZE.

You got it.

OSHOOSI SIZE.

(Singing.)

OGUN SIZE.

Playing back up and doing temptation moves,

OSHOOSI SIZE.

(Singing.)

Laughing!

OGUN SIZE.

(Cracking up!)

OSHOOSI SIZE.

(Singing.)

OGUN SIZE.

(Smiling.)

OSHOOSI SIZE.

(Singing.)

ELEGBA.

Elegba appears at the window,

like a glimmer of moonlight,

for a moment is gone.

OSHOOSI SIZE.

Oshoosi sees it, How could he not?

He stops singing.

OGUN SIZE.

What happened?

OSHOOSI SIZE.

Tired. Voice tired.

OGUN SIZE.
    C'mon man finish.
OSHOOSI SIZE.
    I can't man.
OGUN SIZE.
    Eh brother just try to …
OSHOOSI SIZE.
    Eh man I'm done …
OGUN SIZE.
    But Oshoo you …
    C'mon man you the star.
    Shine little brother …
OSHOOSI SIZE.
    I don't want to play no more.
OGUN SIZE.
    Brother …
OSHOOSI SIZE.
    Eh, Stop pushing me Og.
    I said I am done man.
    I'm going to bed.
OGUN SIZE.
OSHOOSI SIZE.
    Oshoosi Size exits to bed.
OGUN SIZE.
    Ogun Size is left alone.
    Without his brother.
    The music plays in the background.
OGUN SIZE.
    The music turns off.
    Just the sound of night, now.
OGUN SIZE.
    Okay man. Okay.
    Good night.
OGUN SIZE.
    Ogun Size stands alone in the night.
    Staring.
OGUN SIZE.

OGUN SIZE.

OGUN SIZE.

OGUN SIZE.

OGUN SIZE.

OGUN SIZE.

OGUN SIZE.
And the next morning

Scene 6

OGUN SIZE.
Ogun Size enters
Osi!
OGUN SIZE.
Calling for his brother
Osi …
Oshoosi Size!
OSHOOSI SIZE.
Waking up, coming in
Og man
Why you calling?
OGUN SIZE.
Get up.
OSHOOSI SIZE.
What time is it?
OGUN SIZE.
Time to go.
OSHOOSI SIZE.
Eh man, look …
OGUN SIZE.
Get up!
OSHOOSI SIZE.
The court house open 'til bout five today.

OGUN SIZE.

You gotta go.

OSHOOSI SIZE.

It ain't even five in the morning yet.

OGUN SIZE.

I said get it up!

OSHOOSI SIZE.

What you talking about man?

What you doin?

OGUN SIZE.

THROW

OSHOOSI SIZE.

Eh man that's all my shit!

OGUN SIZE.

Get it together …

OSHOOSI SIZE.

Why you …

Ogun why you doing this brother?

OGUN SIZE.

Let's go!

OSHOOSI SIZE.

Brother … Brother Size man …

OGUN SIZE.

You got to get outta here.

OSHOOSI SIZE.

You just …

You upset!

What you mad at?

What, you don't believe me?

Og!

Ogun!

Man … don't do me like this!

OGUN SIZE.

Get your shit. Get in the truck.

OSHOOSI SIZE.

Og.

OGUN SIZE.

Don't come back.

Don't call here.

Don't write …

When they come here …
When the law comes here for you …
I'm going to deny you …
They gone ask for my brother …
I'm going to say I ain't got none …
He gone say there two Size',
I'm gone say nah, just one. Only one …
I'm a deny you …
Up to three times …
That's all I can take. That's how many times I can do it …
Don't cry when you hear about it …
Don't think I don't know you …
Don't believe it …
Hear me …
You here with me …
Always …
But you gotta go 'fore you get caught …
Get in the truck, all your shit brother …
Everything you need …
Need Shoosi need …
Only stop when you need …
So don't stop til you free …
Don't stop …
Open your hand.

OSHOOSI SIZE.
What!

OGUN SIZE.
Open your hand!

OSHOOSI SIZE.
Okay …

OGUN SIZE.
This it …
This everything …
All I got it's yours.
Here Oshoosi.

OSHOOSI SIZE.
Og man don't do this …

OGUN SIZE.
It's done …
Get in the truck …

Take it … Go south … See Mexico.
OSHOOSI SIZE.
   Mexico …
OGUN SIZE.
   It's right there and you ain't never been … right?
OSHOOSI SIZE.

OGUN SIZE.
   What you waiting on man?
OSHOOSI SIZE.

OGUN SIZE.
   Man don't let them put you back in there.
   I wanna know you still my brother somewhere …
   Anywhere in the world.
   You still my brother …
   I swear.
   Out there you will still be a Size, Oshoosi Size
   Brother to Ogun.
OSHOOSI SIZE.

OGUN SIZE.
   I fixed the truck for you.
   If it act up on you,
   If it start bucking don't stop,
   Hit it and call my name.
   The truck know me …
   It'll carry you on …
OSHOOSI SIZE.
   Oshoosi Size breaking down …
OGUN SIZE.
   Ogun trying to hold it.
   It's alright …
   It's alright brother.
   It's gone be alright.
   I believe you.
   I do.
   Just go.
   Go find you.
   When you meet him,

Ask him if he remember me.
Ask him.
Ask.
OSHOOSI SIZE.

OGUN SIZE.

OSHOOSI SIZE.

OGUN SIZE.

OSHOOSI SIZE.
    Oshoosi Size leaves his brother Ogun Size
    standing in the early morning …
OGUN SIZE.
    Ogun Size sees it, how can he not, and is left alone in the
    early foreday in the morning mist.

End of Play

PROPERTY LIST

Soda
Wrench
Dinner plates
Car keys
Shovel
Radio
Suitcase, clothes
Money

SOUND EFFECTS

Music

NOTES
(Use this space to make notes for your production)